# Home is

Amy Kneeland

BookLeaf Publishing

India | USA | UK

Presentation by *BookLeaf Publishing*

Web: www.bookleafpub.com

E-mail: info@bookleafpub.com

ISBN: 9789358311310

First edition 2023

*To my loving husband and our lovely, furry family.*

# Scooter

I keep one eye on that bottom drawer
while you cook, while you eat, while you clean
It may look like I'm asleep but I know
every time you open a drawer
I'm ready
I know
you will
eventually
Open the bottom drawer
and now both eyes are open and my neck
Disappears
just like me
because the garbage bags
SNAP
CRINKLE
SNAP
It is so scary I don't know why you do it
But you always do so I will leave
an explosion of fur running out of the room

You found me playing in a plastic grocery bag
this morning
I love the noise it makes when I dive inside
Gather it between my feet
Rustle, crinkle, swish
This is obviously not the same thing.

# Scooter

I sit in the window all day.
I watch flies and bees
a bird
I nap while the sun stretches across my belly.
I keep my nose pressed to the glass.
I hear steps.
I see you walk up the path.
Then I am gone
so that when you open
the door
I am already screaming
Youleftmehereallday

# Rocky

Hello.
Hello?
Hello. HELLO. Hello? hello
Helloooooooooooo
Hello? This bathroom is too small.
I would rather be with you. Hello.
Please open this door. hello.
Hello!

HELLO

Oh you are here! Hello hello.
Can I come with you? hello.
The spicy cat does not scare me.
She looks nice.
Hello. You seem nicer.

Hello. I will stay here under the bed.
Because I lied. hello.
The world is scary.
hello.
so I will wait here for you,
under the bed.
hello.
and when you get here,

you will know how happy I am
even though you can't see me
because I purr as loud as that car next door,
and I say
Hello.

# Scooter

What. Is. That.
I guess he's cute.
He smells.
Please send him home.

This is... his home?
Are you sure?
If I lock him in the closet
will it still be his home?
If I hiss at him
will it still be his home?

I'll let him out the window.
The one with the loose screen.
There. He's gone.
No, no, it's good.
Home is you and me.

He came back.
He thinks this is his home.
He thinks you and me are home.

He is a stinky boy.
If he stays, he must understand
It's me

then you
then him.

I don't think he cares
Maybe he doesn't understand.

He wants to play.
He thinks we're friends.

Home is
you
and me

and a stinky boy kitten.

# Scooter

I can't believe
you chose a human
with dogs.

They are vile,
disgusting,
too big.
They stink
worse than Rocky.

Two days is too long
to sleep without you.

Who knows what
those dogs are doing to you?

I will keep you safe.

I will break out.
Sneak up the stairs
in the dead of night.

What is this thing here?
A gate at the door.

One of the resident cats,
another stinky boy,
jumped over it.
That seemed uncomfortable.

I will push through
with the force of my will!
I WILL watch over you this night!

Scary dogs be damned--
They will not lay one paw on you!

# Sparta

They come.
Two new felines
and a lady.

They will not
infiltrate our defenses!
Molon labe!

I will win them over
with my charms.

The lady is acceptable.
She feeds me,
talks to me.
She may stay.

The fire kitten
is an abomination.
I will keep my distance.
She thinks she is human, too.
Nothing but trouble.

The big kitten
will sit in peace
with me.

Together
we are the defense
against flies,
spiders,
and woodpeckers.
We will prevail.

# Kit Kat

Sometimes outside.
Sometimes inside.

I used to rule this place.
There was a coup.
The others try to keep me
under house arrest.
But I have one thing
they do not-
I am allowed outside.

I patrol the neighborhood.
I am the matriarch.
It is my duty to scout

Until the raccoons discovered my food.
Now I have a palace
worthy of me.
A space dedicated
only to me.

Clearly I am still the queen of this house.

# Dogs

FREYA
I have a new best friend.
I am so excited
for a new best friend.

My old best friend is gone.
I miss him.
But it will be better now
with a new best friend.

Together

we can run
as fast as we can

we can find squeakers
in the most clever of toys

we can go on walks

and at the end of the day

we snuggle.

ENDER

There are so many good things here.
My new best friend.
My new humans.
My new cats.
We will all be best, best friends.

# Scooter

How dare you.

This thing is worse
than Rocky.

It wants to be friends.

It is clumsy
and stupid
and drools.
It wants to sniff
Everything.
It has
No manners.
I have to slap it
To make it leave.
It always comes back.
I now give it
A warning cry
When it comes near.
Never forget Dog,
I'm in charge here.

# Freya

BEST DAY EVER.
Five days in a row!

We are in a car
all day.
All of us.
We get to smell so many new things.

There are treats.
A comfy car bed.
Moving pictures out the window.
I can even
sneak kisses
to the humans.

It is simply
the best.

# Kit Kat

For days
you have carried me
in my own palanquin
surrounded by the peasants.

I know
I am meant to be
an inspiration.

Though it be taxing
I will
sing the song of my people
the entire time
the wagon is engaged
to comfort the others.

# Ender

It's hot.
The ground moves.
It's alarming
how fast it goes.
The giant boxes
we pass
are scary.
It makes me
breathe faster.

You say I should enjoy this.
Freya loves it.
Scooter loves it.
But when you open the window
I am afraid
I'll be sucked outside.

I like to be
close to you.
I am glad
we are all together.
But this is scary.

One of the cats
won't stop crying.

I wish
to tell her
it will be okay.

But I don't
know that.

So I will just try
to sleep
through the next
five days.

# Sparta

We now live in a palace,
the toms
separated from
the mollys.

Except for the abomination
the fire kitten
who follows the lady
like a shadow.

But the toms
are Warriors.
We will
guard this house
and rule with grace
until the idiot junior warrior
starts yelling again.

He is obnoxious.
Belligerent.
Demanding.

He must be shown
the true path
of a warrior.

# Rocky

HELLLLLOOOOO
HELLO
Hello

You're here.
Let me tell you about last night.
hello.

There were ghosts to chase,
and then they chased me.
I ran up the stairs
to call them.
I ran down the stairs
when they answered.

Hello, hello.
Are you listening?
You stopped touching me
so I wasn't sure.
Hello.

Hello.
I'm sorry but I will need
to sit on you
look you in the eye

hello
while you pet me
hello
to make sure.

Hello.
I can't help it.
Like that piece of hair
I see right now
on your shoulder
I just
need
to
check--
HELLO

# Kit Kat

The tower
is my domain.
My servants
bring me
the greatest delicacies.
Even the dogs
serve me here.

My royal coat
has come in with new shine
and is so soft.

I am finally recognized
as the queen I am,
descended from gods.

# Scooter

Mom.
Mom.
Mom.
I am trying
to politely tap you
but if you do not wake up
I will bite you.

MOM.
I warned you.
Please follow.
Don't turn over.
MOM.
Follow.
I need you to stand here
while I eat a snack.
Don't leave.
Wait.
Come back.
MOM.
I told you
I need a snack.
Watch me eat my snack.
Okay I'm done.
We can go back to bed.

Wait.
Mom.
Please tuck me in.
I need you to hold
the blanket.
Thank you.
You are the best mom.
I need to hold your hand
in my teeth
to show you so.

# Ender

I am so happy
You came home.
To celebrate
this grand occasion
I will grab your spare shoe
and take it to Dad
to announce
your arrival.
I am
such a good boy.

I am so happy
you came to bed
I will lay on top
of you
to show you
I am such
a good boy.

I am so happy
you are awake
I will roll
feverishly
on you
on the pillow

on Freya
to show you
I am a good boy.

I am so happy.

# Freya

There are dogs.
Did you know
There are other dogs
Outside?
There's a dog.
There's a person.
How dare that house
open its mouth to us!
There's another dog.
And a truck.
The truck is invading!
I will protect you
But the dogs!
Other dogs!
I want to see
The other dogs!
If I keep quiet
And give you
Eeyore eyes
Can I go Outside and meet
the other dogs?

# Rocky

The middle of the night
is dark.
It's the best time
of night
but no one else
thinks so.
It's the best time
to run
Hello

to sing
Hello

The stairs
are the best place
to sing.
The acoustics
are amazing.
No one appreciates
my midnight concerts.
Hello.

# Scooter

Sideways
I dance
Sideways

From the top
of the stairs

Do you dare
to engage?
Sideways

Engage.
Down the stairs
A blur

My eyes are
Black Holes

Around the house
Twice

From the bottom
of the first floor
to the top
of the tallest cat tree

on the second floor.

Sideways
Disengage.
Bite.

# Naps

The windows
are full
of melting cats.
Spilling out of pillows
Dripping off the sills
Toe beans
floating in the air.

The couch
is full
of dogs.
Bellies up
Snoring
like a chainsaw.

When the heat
becomes too much
a sack of fur
Drags itself to the tile
to become a puddle.

We own puddles.
Home is puddles.
Great puddles of love.

www.ingramcontent.com/pod-product-compliance
Lightning Source LLC
LaVergne TN
LVHW021330200726

843509LV00014B/2479